Nature's Red Flags

Written by Kerrie Shanahan

Flying Start
to Literacy®

T0342923

Contents

Introduction

Imagine walking through a rainforest . . . Tall trees, twisting vines and ancient ferns surround you. The sound of birds and insects fills the air. Water bubbles over a rocky riverbed.

Now imagine you are told that many frogs in this forest are dying. The forest looks healthy, so why would this happen? What does it mean?

Some animals, like frogs, are super **sensitive** to changes where they live. They are the first animals in the **habitat** to be affected, and the changes can lead to large numbers getting sick and dying.

Sudden changes to a group of animals send an early warning to scientists. They tell them that something is not right. Is the water polluted? Is the climate changing?

Scientists can act on these warnings. They can investigate what is wrong, and search for ways to fix the problems.

Chapter 1

Warning: Pollution

Pollution affects animals. Pollution happens when gases, chemicals or waste get into the land, air or water in an environment.

Pollution can make animals sick and stop them from growing. It can even kill them.

Some animals, like frogs and dragonflies, are affected more quickly than others.

By studying these animals, scientists can find out what is happening. Then they can try to solve the problem before other animals are affected.

Pollution: A problem for poison frogs

Poison frogs are brightly coloured frogs that live in wet, tropical rainforests. Some poison frogs are in danger of dying out, and pollution is one of the reasons why.

Pollution in the rainforests where these frogs live comes from nearby farms, factories, towns and villages. It ends up in rivers and streams, and in the fog and mist that surround the forest.

A tiny killer

The golden poison frog has enough venom to kill ten people. It is only about as big as a paper clip.

Poison frogs are very **sensitive** to pollution. Like all frogs, they take in water through their skin. This means that chemicals in the air and water easily get into their bodies.

These chemicals can make the frogs sick, and can even kill them.

Life cycle of a frog

Most frogs lay their eggs in water. But many types of poison frogs lay their eggs on land, on the forest floor. These jellylike eggs easily absorb **pollutants** that are in the air. Sometimes this causes the eggs not to hatch.

When the eggs do hatch, the adult frogs carry the tadpoles on their backs to tiny pools of water that sit on the leaves of plants. If this water is not clean and fresh, the tadpoles may get sick or die, and do not develop into frogs.

An adult frog carries its tadpoles on its back.

A healthy habitat can be the home for many frogs.

Scientists study poison frog populations because they are often the first animals in their **habitat** affected by pollution.

If the number of frogs is high, then this tells scientists that the habitat is healthy. But if the number of frogs is low, then something may be wrong.

Scientists can then work on ways to protect the habitat before it is too badly damaged.

Protecting dragonflies

Dragonflies have been on Earth for a very long time – since before the dinosaurs! But many dragonflies have been dying, and pollution is one of the reasons.

Life cycle of the dragonfly

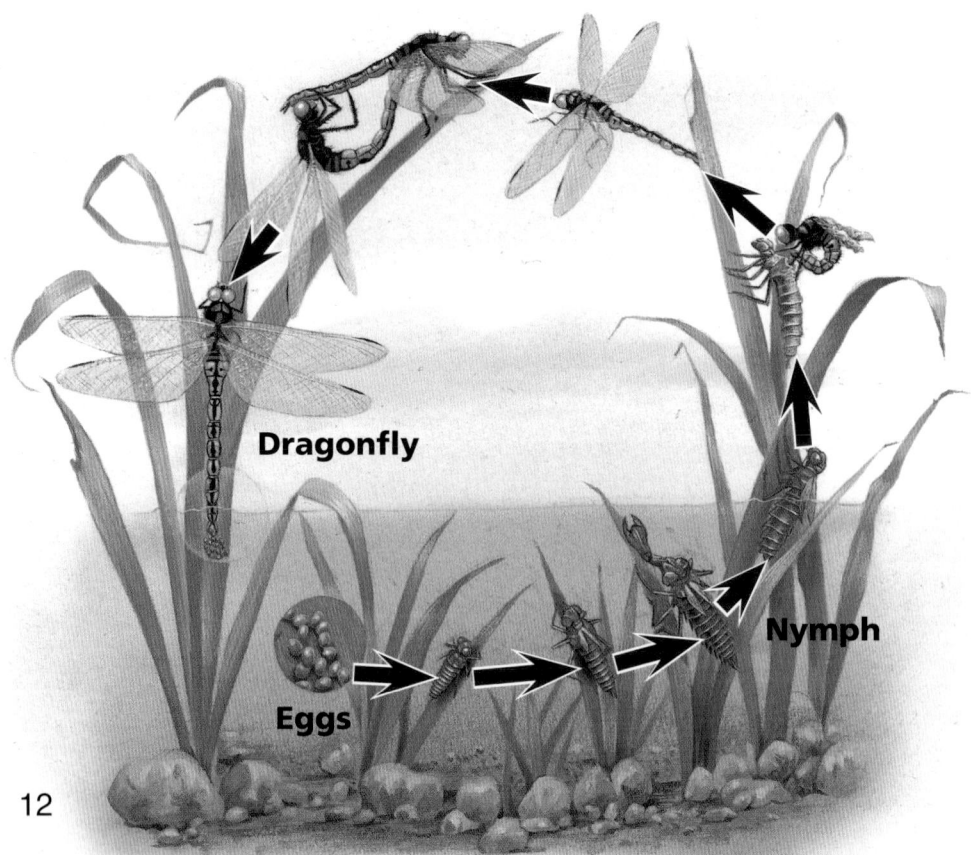

Dragonfly

Nymph

Eggs

Female dragonflies lay eggs on plants in ponds, swamps and wetlands. Dragonfly **larva**, called nymphs, hatch from the eggs. Nymphs live underwater, and they need clean, fresh water to survive.

After a month or more of growing, the nymphs crawl out of the water onto plants. Then they shed their skins and become adult dragonflies. The right types of healthy plants are needed for this to happen.

In England, scientists noticed that some types of dragonflies were in danger of becoming **extinct**. They discovered that pollution from farms, factories and homes was ending up in the water, air and soil where dragonflies live.

These chemicals affect the number of eggs an adult dragonfly lays, and whether a nymph develops into a dragonfly.

The nymph sheds its skin and becomes an adult dragonfly.

One group of people decided to do something about the problem. They set up a dragonfly centre within a nature reserve called Wicken Fen.

The dragonfly centre has two large ponds. These ponds are kept clean so that the dragonflies have a healthy habitat where they can breed and lay their eggs – and where nymphs can grow. This is helping to increase dragonfly numbers. There are 22 different **species** of dragonflies living in the nature reserve.

Volunteers at the centre teach people about dragonflies and take visitors on guided tours.

Chapter 2

Warning: Dangerous pesticides

Farmers have a problem. Insects like to eat their crops. Some farmers use chemicals called **pesticides** to protect their crops from insects. Farmers spray pesticides onto crops, or coat the seeds of plants with them. The pesticides stop insects from eating the crops.

For a long time, many people thought that pesticides were safe. But some animals such as bees and birds have been badly affected by them.

Dying bees cause laws to change

Did you know that if there were no bees, there would be fewer plants for us to eat?

Bees are responsible for **pollinating** 70 per cent of all the plants we eat. Pollinators are animals that transfer pollen from one plant to another so that the plant can reproduce – and new plants can grow.

Over the past 20 years, scientists noticed that large numbers of bees have died. They investigated and found out that some pesticides were killing bees.

Scientists discovered that if bees drink water that has these **pesticides** in it, the bees might die. Even if the bees survive, the pesticides damage their **nervous system**. When this happens, the bees cannot find their way back to their hive, and they die anyway.

Sometimes, pesticides sprayed onto crops are carried to other places by the wind. The chemicals can land on plants that bees visit. These bees then carry pollen from the plants back to their hive. The pesticides on the pollen kill lots of bees in the hive.

When scientists discovered that some types of pesticides were killing bees, they took action. In many places around the world, these pesticides have now been banned. In other places, rules have been changed so that these pesticides are used in a safer way.

Chapter 3

Warning: Global warming

The earth is getting hotter and this rise in temperature is making it difficult for some animals to survive.

Pikas send scientists a warning

High up in the mountains of North America lives the American pika, a small furry mammal. Pikas have very thick fur, which helps them stay warm when it is cold. But in warm weather, pikas can easily overheat and die.

If the **habitat** where pikas live is getting warmer and staying warmer for longer, then the pika could be in trouble.

Scientists monitor changes in the numbers of pikas in an area, to find out if global warming is having an impact.

Pikas are good animals for scientists to study because they are **sensitive** to changes in temperature. They are also easy for scientists to observe because they are active during the day and make loud, high-pitched cries, and they leave lots of droppings.

Scientists monitor the numbers of pikas living in an area, and compare this to the numbers that once lived there. They also check the change in temperature in these places during this time.

They have discovered that in some places where pikas once lived, there are now no pikas at all. And it is warmer now than it once was in these places.

Scientists also found out that many pikas are now living higher up mountains than ever before. Scientists believe that pikas are moving higher and higher in search of cooler temperatures.

This research showed scientists that climate change is one reason pika numbers are declining.

Scientists are using what they know about pikas to help other animals that might soon be affected by climate change, too.

Conclusion

Some of our actions have been harming the environment. We are using pesticides and creating pollution, and our use of fossil fuels is causing temperatures to rise. Some animals have been badly affected by this – their numbers have dropped and this has sent warnings to scientists.

The good news is that we have listened to these warnings and we are making changes to help the environment.

So the next time you hear frogs croaking and bees buzzing – or you see dragonflies flitting around and fish darting in streams, you will know that their **habitat** is doing well!

Glossary

extinct not existing anymore

habitat the natural home of a plant or animal

larva the first stage of an insect's life

nervous system a system of nerves, including the brain and spinal cord

pesticides an agent used to destroy pests

pollinating fertilising a plant with pollen

pollutants substances that cause pollution

prehistoric the time before written records were kept

sensitive easily affected by something

sheds to lose skin or a shell

species a group of living things that are very similar

Index